OUR SOLAR SYSTEM

THE SUN
THE CENTER OF OUR SOLAR SYSTEM

by Mari Schuh

pogo

Ideas for Parents and Teachers

Pogo Books let children practice reading informational text while introducing them to nonfiction features such as headings, labels, sidebars, maps, and diagrams, as well as a table of contents, glossary, and index.

Carefully leveled text with a strong photo match offers early fluent readers the support they need to succeed.

Before Reading

- "Walk" through the book and point out the various nonfiction features. Ask the student what purpose each feature serves.
- Look at the glossary together. Read and discuss the words.

Read the Book

- Have the child read the book independently.
- Invite him or her to list questions that arise from reading.

After Reading

- Discuss the child's questions. Talk about how he or she might find answers to those questions.
- Prompt the child to think more. Ask: The Sun is the only star in our solar system. Did you know this before reading this book? What more would you like to learn about the Sun?

Pogo Books are published by Jump!
5357 Penn Avenue South
Minneapolis, MN 55419
www.jumplibrary.com

Copyright © 2023 Jump!
International copyright reserved in all countries. No part of this book may be reproduced in any form without written permission from the publisher.

Library of Congress Cataloging-in-Publication Data is available at www.loc.gov or upon request from the publisher.

ISBN: 979-8-88524-370-4 (hardcover)
ISBN: 979-8-88524-371-1 (paperback)
ISBN: 979-8-88524-372-8 (ebook)

Editor: Jenna Gleisner
Designer: Emma Bersie

Photo Credits: Travel4U/Shutterstock, cover (background); Triff/Shutterstock, cover (Sun); robert_s/Shutterstock, 1; LIGHT_ONLY/Shutterstock, 3; Computer Earth/Shutterstock, 4; NASA/Goddard/SDO, 5; Goinyk Production/Shutterstock, 6-7; muratart/Shutterstock, 8-9; MA.Turcotte/Shutterstock, 10; Vladimir Arndt/Shutterstock, 11; Piotr Krzeslak/Shutterstock, 12-13; Withan Tor/Shutterstock, 14-15; NASA/SOFIA/Lynette Cook, 16-17; ESA/NASA/SOHO, 18; Science History Images/Alamy, 19; NASA/Johns Hopkins APL/Steve Gribben, 20-21; NASA images/Shutterstock, 23.

Printed in the United States of America at Corporate Graphics in North Mankato, Minnesota.

For Paige

TABLE OF CONTENTS

CHAPTER 1
Hot, Spinning Star..............................4

CHAPTER 2
The Center of Our Solar System.............10

CHAPTER 3
Amazing Discoveries..........................18

ACTIVITIES & TOOLS
Try This!.......................................22
Glossary..23
Index...24
To Learn More.................................24

CHAPTER 1

· ·

HOT, SPINNING STAR

The Sun is a **star**. It is the closest star to Earth. But it is still 93 million miles (150 million kilometers) away. It would take a car going 60 miles (97 km) per hour 175 years to reach the Sun.

Sun ·····

The Sun is a glowing ball of hot gases. The gases are always moving. They can shoot out from the Sun. These are called solar flares. They are explosions of energy.

solar flare

The Sun spins, like **planets** do. But the Sun is not solid. Parts of it spin at different speeds. At the Sun's **equator**, one full spin takes about 25 Earth days. The Sun spins slower at its **poles**. There, one full spin takes 36 Earth days.

DID YOU KNOW?

There are millions of stars in the **universe**. But they are not in our **solar system**. The Sun is the only star in our solar system.

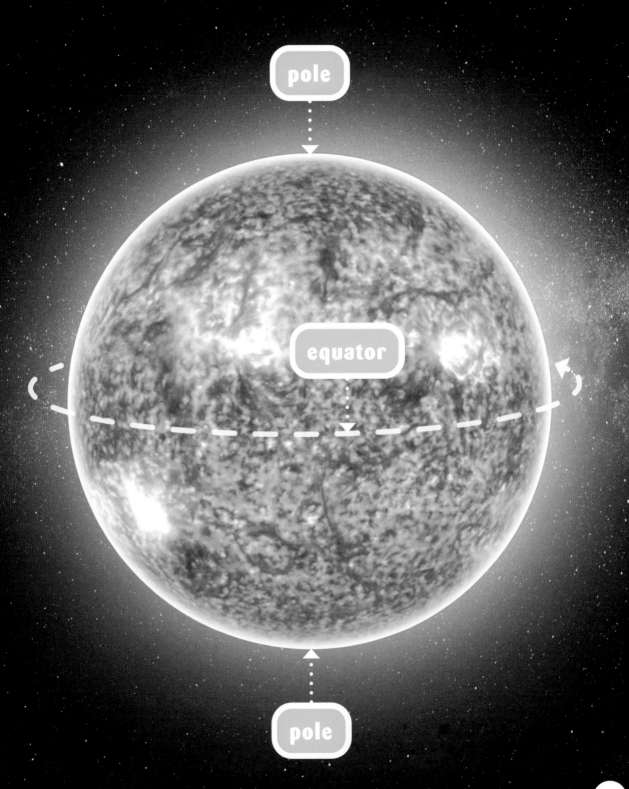

The Sun is hot! Its surface temperature is about 10,000 degrees Fahrenheit (5,500 degrees Celsius). Its **core** is even hotter. How hot? Temperatures reach 27 million degrees Fahrenheit (15 million degrees Celsius)!

TAKE A LOOK!

What are the Sun's layers? Take a look!

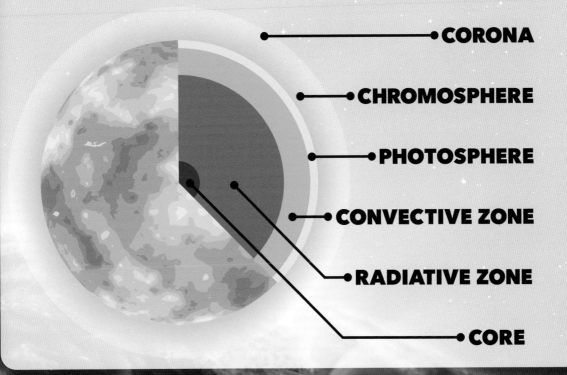

- CORONA
- CHROMOSPHERE
- PHOTOSPHERE
- CONVECTIVE ZONE
- RADIATIVE ZONE
- CORE

CHAPTER 2

THE CENTER OF OUR SOLAR SYSTEM

The Sun shines bright. It is the brightest object in Earth's daytime sky.

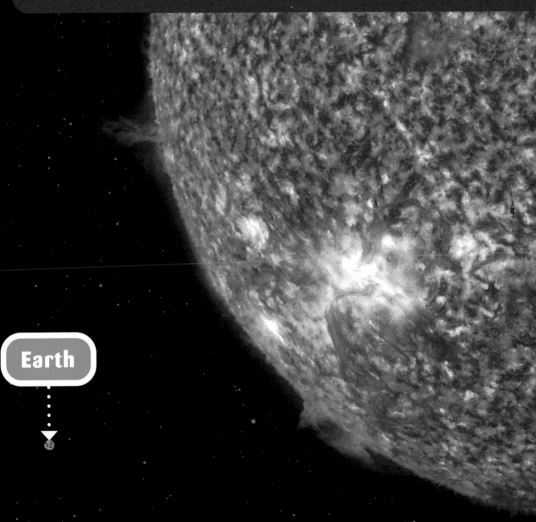

The Sun may look small from Earth. But it is huge. About 1 million Earths could fit inside the Sun!

Earth

sunlight

Life on Earth needs the Sun's light and heat. It depends on it. Without it, plants couldn't grow. People and animals need plants to eat.

The Sun's heat warms Earth. Without it, Earth would freeze. Plants, animals, and people could not survive.

DID YOU KNOW?

Light and heat from the Sun travel far to reach us. It takes sunlight about eight minutes to reach Earth.

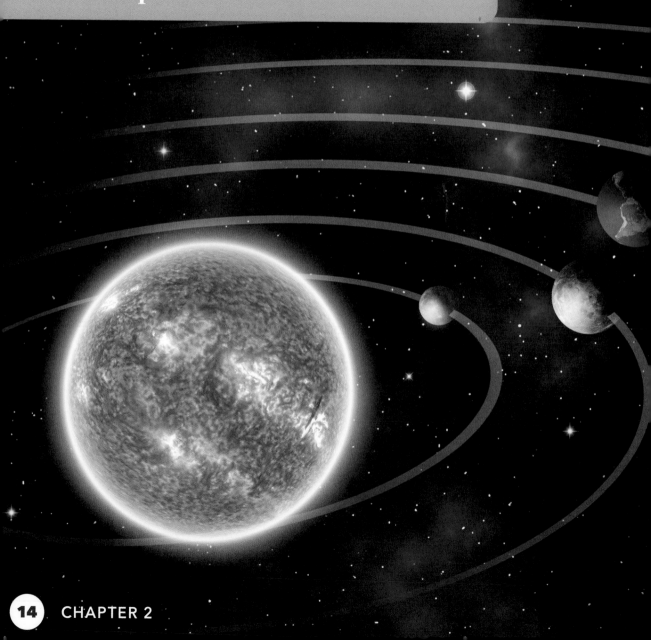

The Sun is the center of our solar system. Everything in it **orbits** the Sun. This includes Earth and the other planets.

The Sun is the largest object in our solar system. Take a look!

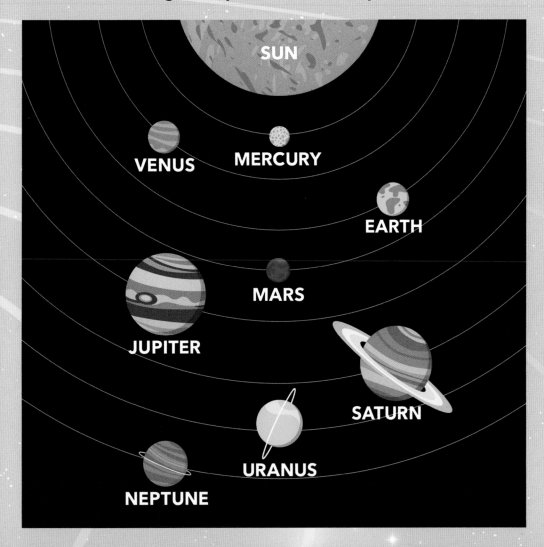

The Sun's **gravity** is very strong. It holds our solar system together. An object's gravity depends on its size, **mass**, and **density**. Let's say you weigh 100 pounds (45 kilograms) on Earth. You would weigh 2,790 pounds (1,266 kg) on the Sun!

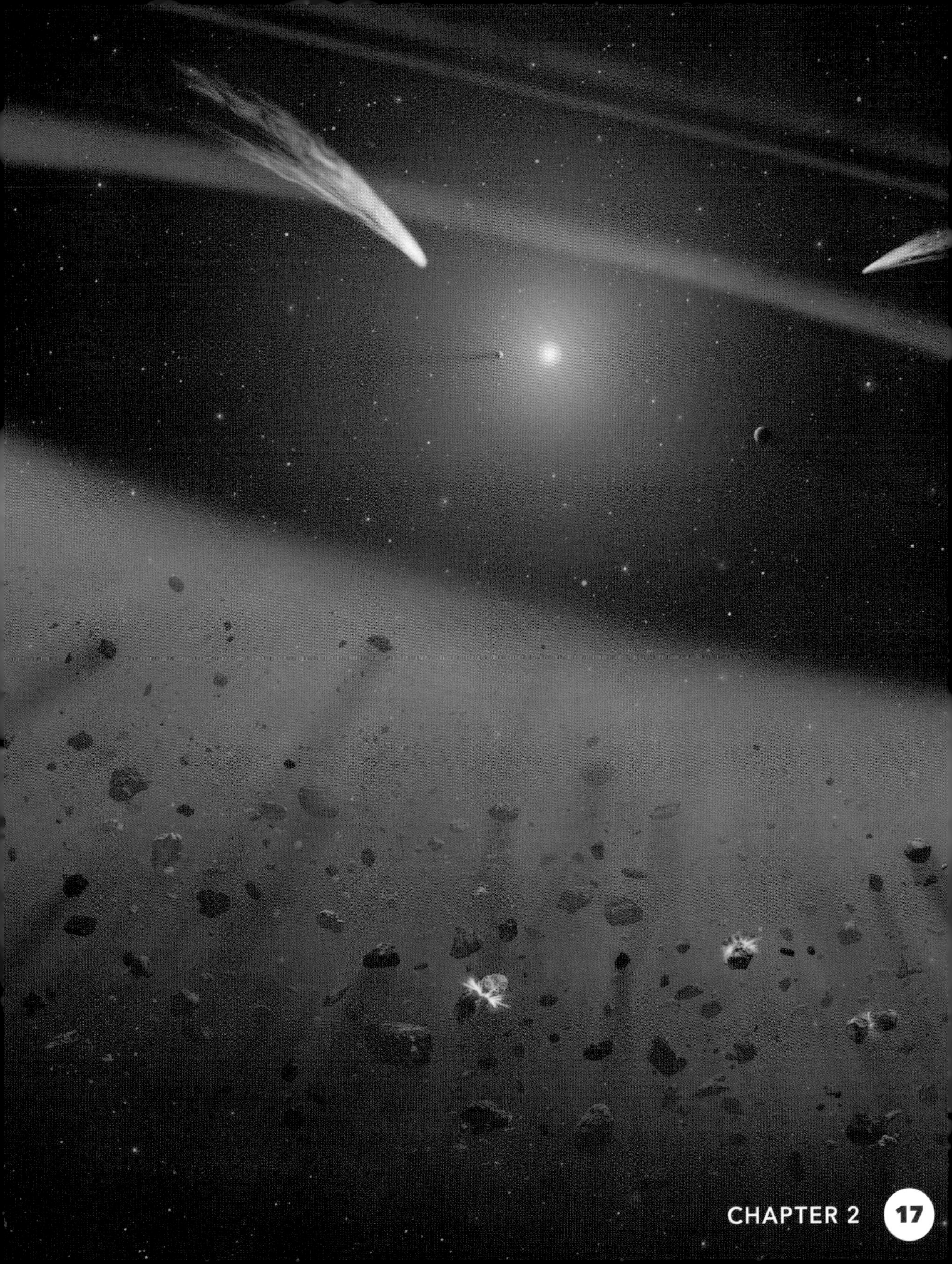

CHAPTER 3

AMAZING DISCOVERIES

In 1995, the *SOHO* **spacecraft** launched into space. It was sent to study the Sun. It has been watching the Sun longer than any other **satellite**. It found **tornadoes** on the Sun's surface. The storms are huge. They are almost as wide as Earth!

SOHO ·····▶

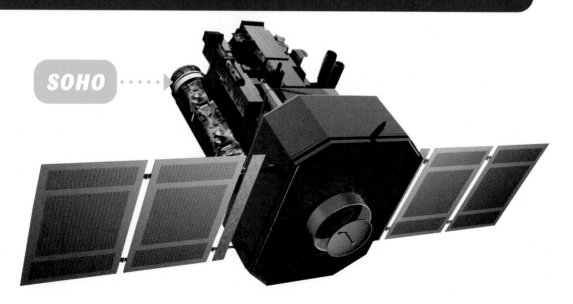

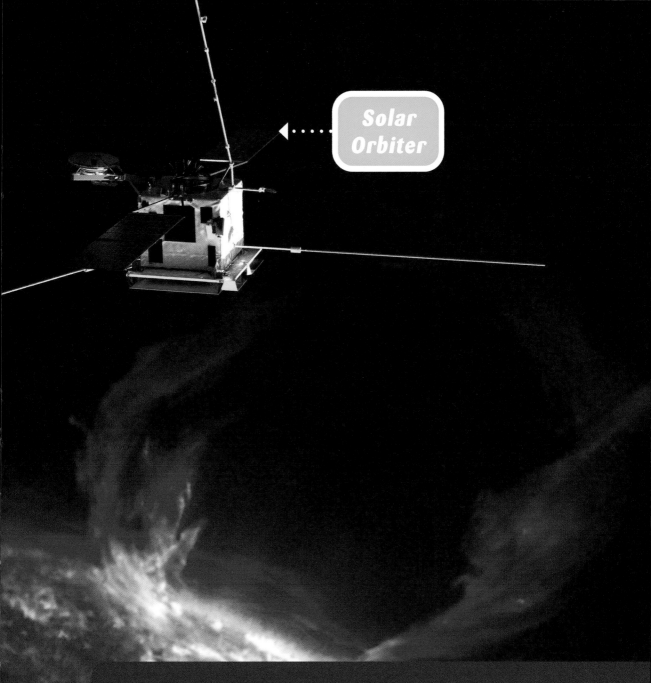

Solar
Orbiter

The *Solar Orbiter* launched in 2020.
It takes photos of the Sun. They are
the closest photos ever taken of the Sun.

The *Parker Solar Probe* is flying closer to the Sun than any other spacecraft. Why? It studies the Sun's **corona**. It is much hotter than its surface. Scientists want to learn why.

The Sun is amazing. Life on Earth depends on it. What more would you like to learn about the Sun?

DID YOU KNOW?

The *Parker Solar Probe* is fast. It travels about 430,000 miles (700,000 km) per hour. That is like traveling from New York to Tokyo, Japan, in less than one minute! *Zoom!*

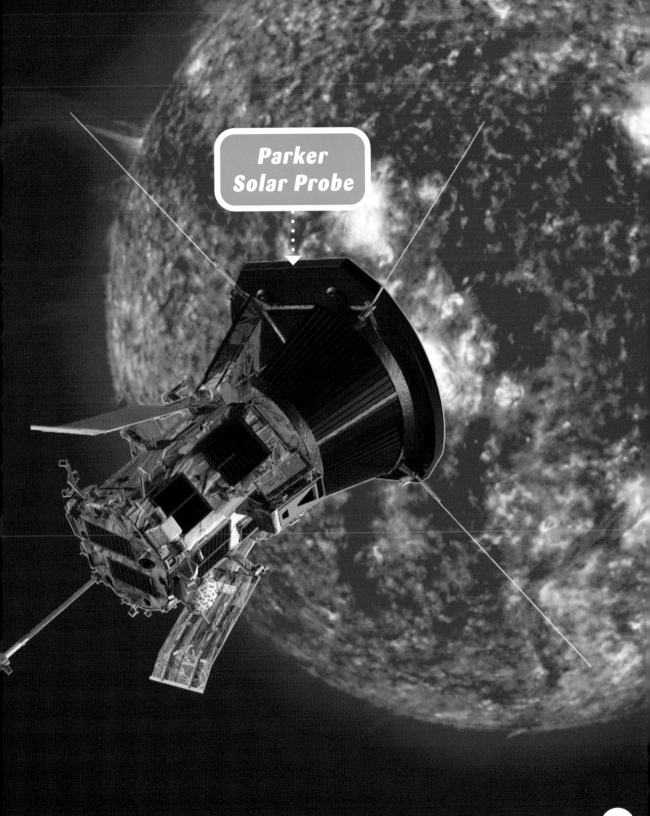

ACTIVITIES & TOOLS

TRY THIS!

SUN IN A BOTTLE

The Sun is made of gases. See how they swirl in this fun activity!

What You Need:
- small, empty plastic bottle with lid
- funnel
- oil, such as olive oil or canola oil
- red food coloring
- cup
- water

1. Use the funnel to fill the bottle about halfway full of oil.

2. Fill a cup with some water. Then mix in red food coloring.

3. Use the funnel to pour the water into the bottle so it is full.

4. Tightly screw the lid on the bottle.

5. Gently shake and swirl the bottle. What do you see? What happens to the colored water and the oil?

GLOSSARY

core: The center, most inner part of the Sun or a planet.

corona: The outermost layer of the Sun.

density: The measure of how heavy or light an object is for its size. Density is measured by dividing an object's mass by its volume.

equator: An imaginary line around the middle of the Sun or a planet.

gravity: The force that pulls things toward the center of a planet or body and keeps them from floating away.

mass: The amount of physical matter an object has.

orbits: Travels in a circular path around something.

planets: Large bodies that orbit, or travel in circles around, the Sun.

poles: The two geographical points that are farthest from the equator.

satellite: A spacecraft that is sent to orbit the Sun, Moon, or planets.

solar system: The Sun, together with its orbiting bodies, such as the planets, their moons, and asteroids, comets, and meteors.

spacecraft: Vehicles that travel in space.

star: A huge ball of burning gas in outer space that creates heat and light.

tornadoes: Violent and destructive windstorms that appear as dark funnel clouds.

universe: All existing matter and space.

INDEX

corona 9, 20

Earth 4, 6, 10, 11, 13, 14, 15, 16, 18, 20

equator 6

gases 5

gravity 16

heat 13

layers 9

life 13, 20

light 13

orbits 14

Parker Solar Probe 20

planets 6, 14, 15

poles 6

shines 10

SOHO 18

solar flares 5

Solar Orbiter 19

solar system 6, 14, 15, 16

spins 6

star 4, 6

temperatures 8

tornadoes 18

universe 6

TO LEARN MORE

Finding more information is as easy as 1, 2, 3.

① **Go to www.factsurfer.com**

② **Enter "Sun" into the search box.**

③ **Choose your book to see a list of websites.**

FACT SURFER